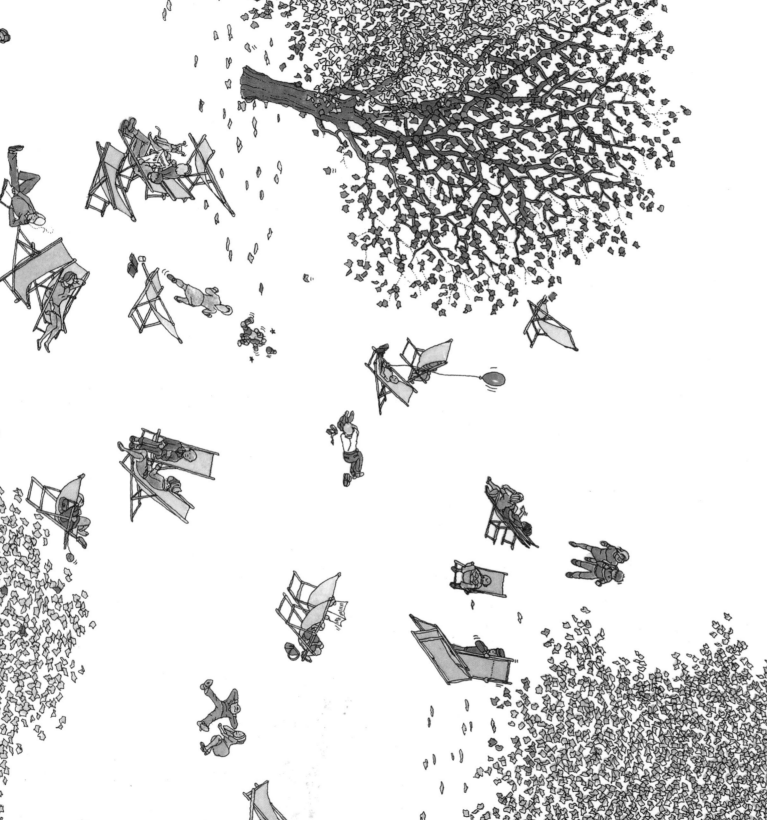

PIERO VENTURA'S BOOK OF

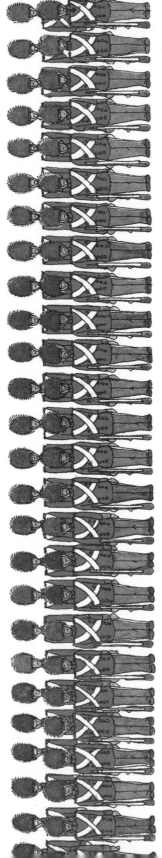

Parade in Copenhagen, Denmark

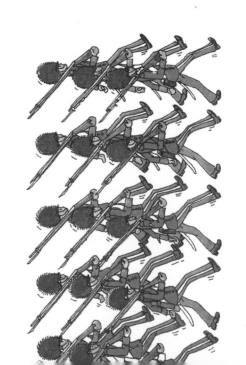

This edition first published in the United States of America in 2009 by
UNIVERSE PUBLISHING
A Division of Rizzoli International Publications, Inc.
300 Park Avenue South
New York, NY 10010
www.rizzoliusa.com

© Piero Ventura, 1975

The publisher gratefully acknowledges
Douglas and Allegra Woods for their efforts
in bringing *Book of Cities* back to print.

2009 2010 2011 2012 2013 / 10 9 8 7 6 5 4 3 2 1

Printed in China
ISBN-13: 978-0-7893-1821-3
Library of Congress Control Number: 2008933181
Cover design: Sara Stemen

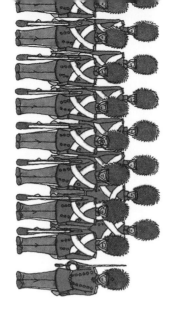

CITIES

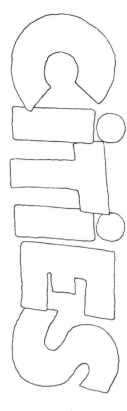

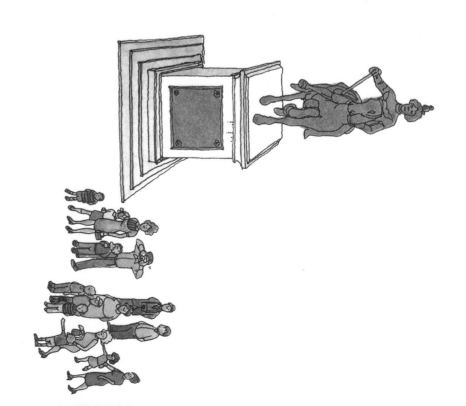

This book is dedicated to my grandchildren
Anna, Francesca, Giovanni, and Primo

From the author's desktop

I've always wished I could fly, ever since I was little. Not by sitting in an airplane, but by flapping my arms like birds flap their wings. I was fascinated by the idea of seeing the world from above— houses, people, cities, the countryside, the sea. Everything must be more beautiful from up there! Of course, I never quite succeeded.

So then I tried to imagine what it would be like, and to tell about it through drawing.

Obviously, from way up high everything looks tinier and more curious, but you can see and understand a lot of things you can't from down on the ground. So, year after year, book after book, more and more young readers all around the world came to call me "the little-people guy."

Over thirty years have now passed since I drew *Book of Cities*. Cities, and children, have changed a lot since then—and naturally I have, too; to see any one of the many "little people" in this book, I now have to put on my glasses! But I'm sure that there are still many little boys and girls all around the globe who want to fly—in order to see and understand a world that is increasingly complicated, yet ever more fascinating.

Piero Ventura

Anghiari, Italy

LIVING IN A CITY

A city is a place where thousands of people live and work. Some people prefer to live in cities because more is happening there. They like the rapid, bustling pace of city life. They enjoy crowds and busy streets. They like the tall buildings and constant activity.

Because cities are crowded, each family cannot have its own house. Many people live in apartment houses. Some of these buildings are so big that hundreds of families live in them. Yet the people who live there often don't know their neighbors as well as they know their friends who live in another, more distant section of the city.

There are also people who do live in houses—sometimes surrounded by a yard and garden. Or they may live in a "row house," which is joined to its neighbor by a common wall. There are even people who live on boats!

You will find big cities in almost every country in the world. All of them are alike as far as being crowded. But they can also be very different. This book shows many of the colorful likenesses and differences that make famous cities so interesting. It also shows how people live in different cities around the world.

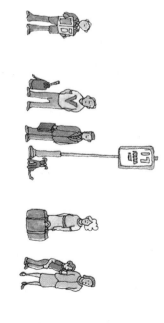

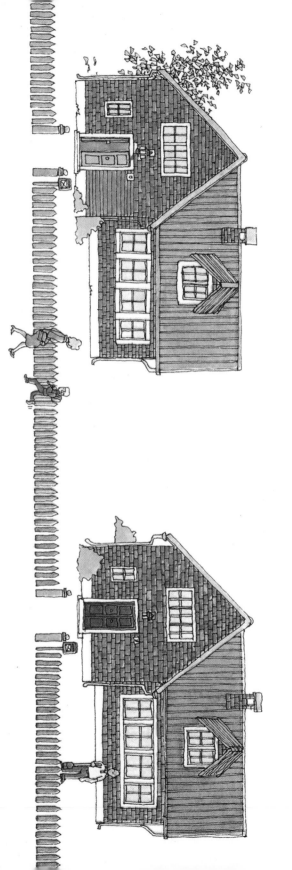

London is one of the world's biggest cities. Located on the River Thames, the capital of the United Kingdom stretches out for miles in every direction. Londoners love their flowers and gardens. Even if they live in a modern high-rise apartment house, they are likely to display a plant on the balcony.

The smallest single-family home usually has a yard with a flower garden, a hedge, and deck chairs for enjoying the sun. The tiniest yards in front of the row houses have shrubs and climbing vines. Here is a pleasant residential section along the river. Incidentally, you will notice that the British drive on the left-hand side of the road.

City people—whether they live in New York or Tokyo—love to be out-doors when the weather is good. This is especially true in Rome in the spring. Rome is the capital of Italy and one of the most beautiful cities in the world. The people who live there are proud of their city and its history.

All Americans who visit Rome go to see the famous Spanish Steps. These steps lead upward in a series of graceful flights to the tall twin spires of the Church of Trinità dei Monti. They are most beautiful in April when banked with pots of bright red and white azaleas. Few visitors to Rome have failed to sit awhile on a step or landing—perhaps to read a letter from home, or to study a map or guidebook.

The Romans spend hours in their outdoor cafés, sipping coffee, talking to friends, and watching the passing traffic. They are among the friendliest people in the world.

Even in Rome, as you can see, children lose their balloons, and policemen give tickets to reckless drivers.

Cities can be cold in the wintertime, and Moscow is one of the coldest. During the winter months, blizzards sweep through the Russian capital, covering the streets and boulevards with snow. Men with shovels and snow plows have to go to work. Horse-drawn sleighs appear. And people bundle up in heavy coats, fur hats, and overshoes. Few cars try to get through the deep drifts.

At the very center of the city, on Red Square, stands St. Basil's Cathedral, one of Russia's most famous buildings. Its amazing domes look like twisted onions and pineapples painted with rainbow colors. Built as a church more than 500 years ago, St. Basil's is now a state historical museum.

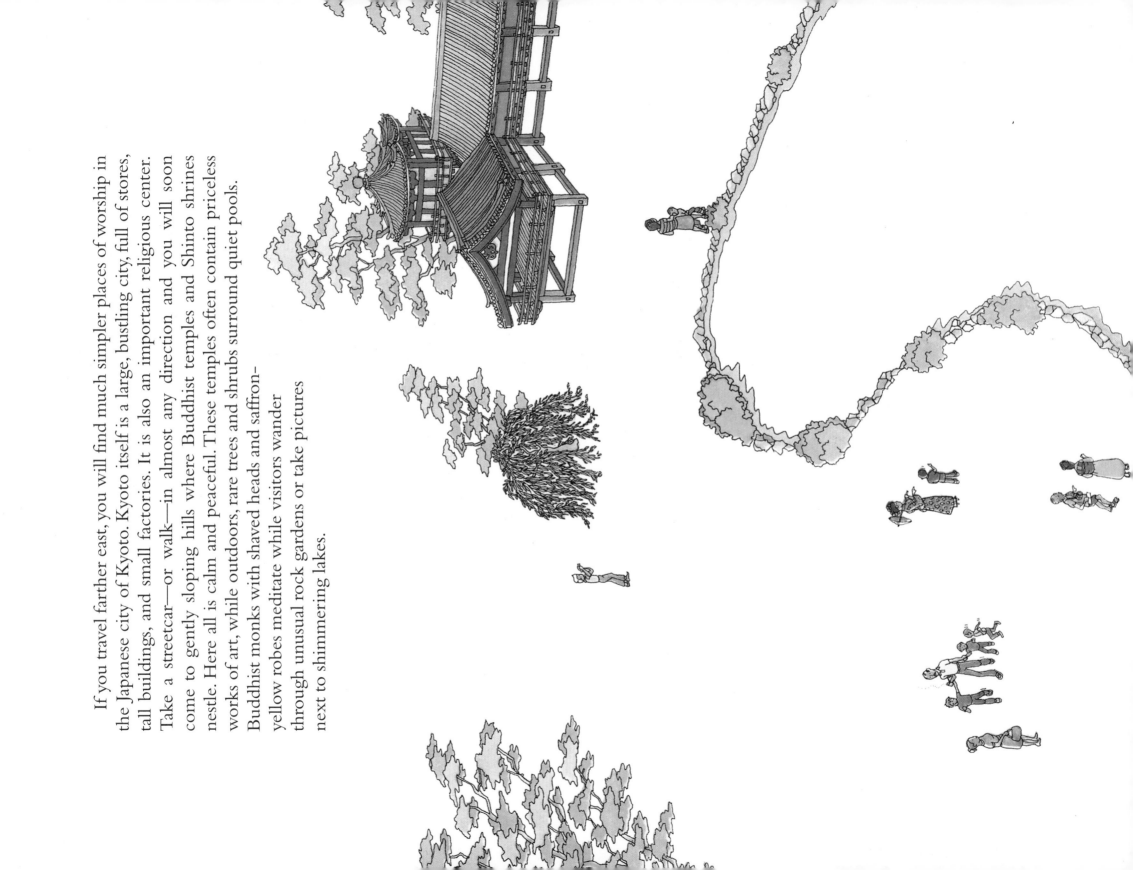

If you travel farther east, you will find much simpler places of worship in the Japanese city of Kyoto. Kyoto itself is a large, bustling city, full of stores, tall buildings, and small factories. It is also an important religious center. Take a streetcar—or walk—in almost any direction and you will soon come to gently sloping hills where Buddhist temples and Shinto shrines nestle. Here all is calm and peaceful. These temples often contain priceless works of art, while outdoors, rare trees and shrubs surround quiet pools. Buddhist monks with shaved heads and saffron-yellow robes meditate while visitors wander through unusual rock gardens or take pictures next to shimmering lakes.

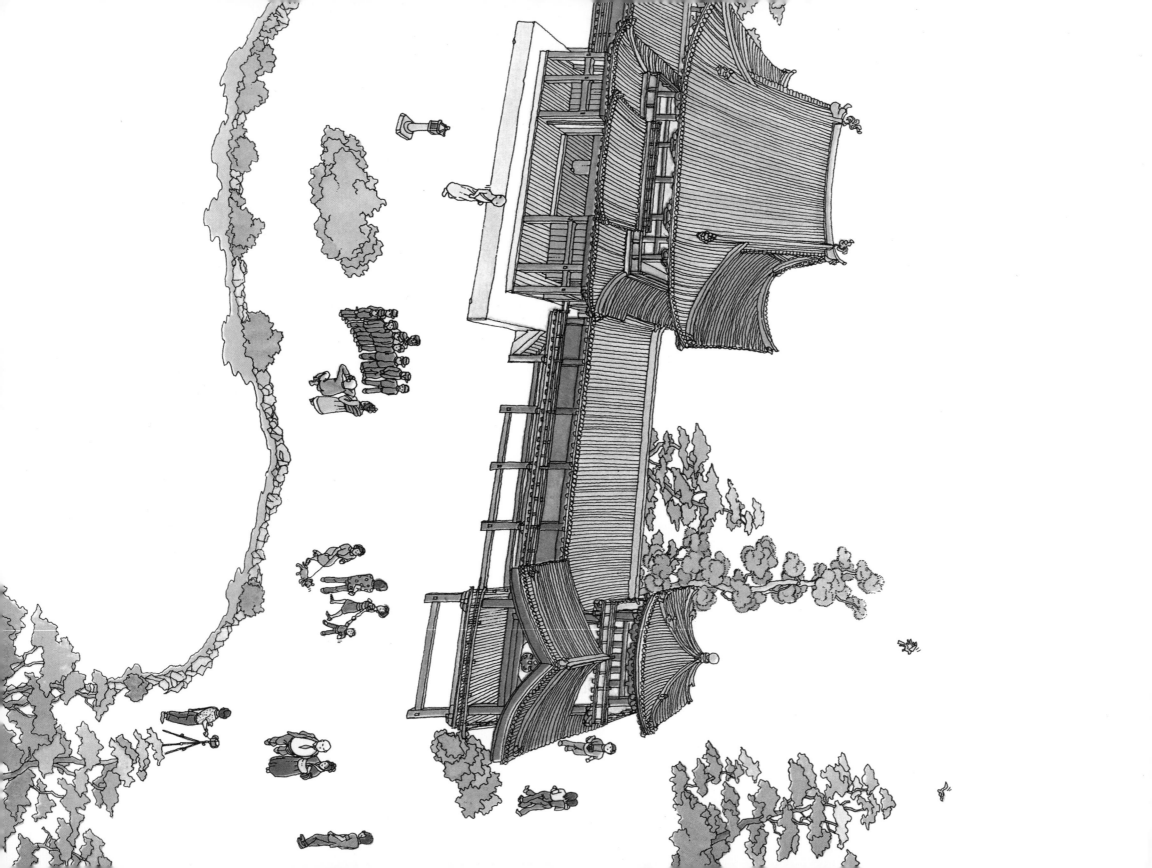

In Amsterdam, people live on houseboats, too. But mainly they live in charming old row houses along the canals that crisscross this great Dutch city. Streets are narrow, paved with cobblestones, and shaded by leafy trees. Storks nest in chimneys, and cats walk on the high gables of the houses.

During rush hour, cars and trucks struggle to get through the crowded streets, but on Sundays everyone takes to bicycles. Bicycles are popular in this city. There are special traffic lanes and red-on-white road signs just for cyclists.

Hundreds of bridges cross the many canals of Amsterdam. No one seems to know just how many there are.

On the island of Hong Kong, also in the Far East, there are "floating cities" where people live on houseboats called sampans. There are restaurants—and even barbershops—on boats. You can eat dinner aboard a sampan and look across the harbor at the modern skyscrapers and towering mountains of the city of Victoria.

Hong Kong is a special administrative region of China. Because so many people are crowded into the cities of Hong Kong, there are not enough houses to go around. That is why many people live on boats. In Hong Kong you can see people traveling in rickshaws, little carriages drawn by men. And skillful weavers sit by the road making baskets out of bamboo.

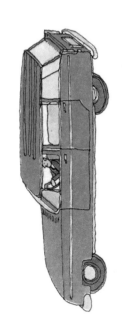

GETTING AROUND IN A CITY

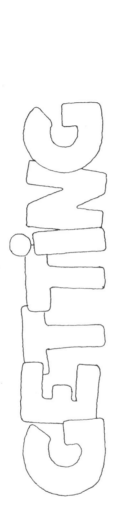

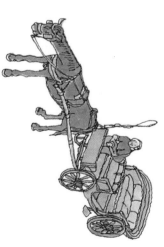

Because cities are so crowded, transportation is usually a real problem. How can so many people get to work? (Often a person lives many miles from the place where he works.) How can enough supplies and food be brought into the city every day?

City streets are always full of traffic. Cars, trucks, buses, and taxicabs fight for space. Trains, boats, and planes are constantly carrying people in and out of the city.

In an effort to get some of the traffic off the streets, more and more cities have introduced underground trains or subways. And usually there are special highways to move cars over and around cities without them getting onto the crowded streets.

Many cities are located at busy ports where ocean-going freighters and passenger ships can easily dock. Others are on rivers and canals, so boats and flat-bottomed barges can provide transportation in and out of the city. And almost always cities are at the center of a complex system of railways.

Cities with good transportation facilities are the ones that become big.

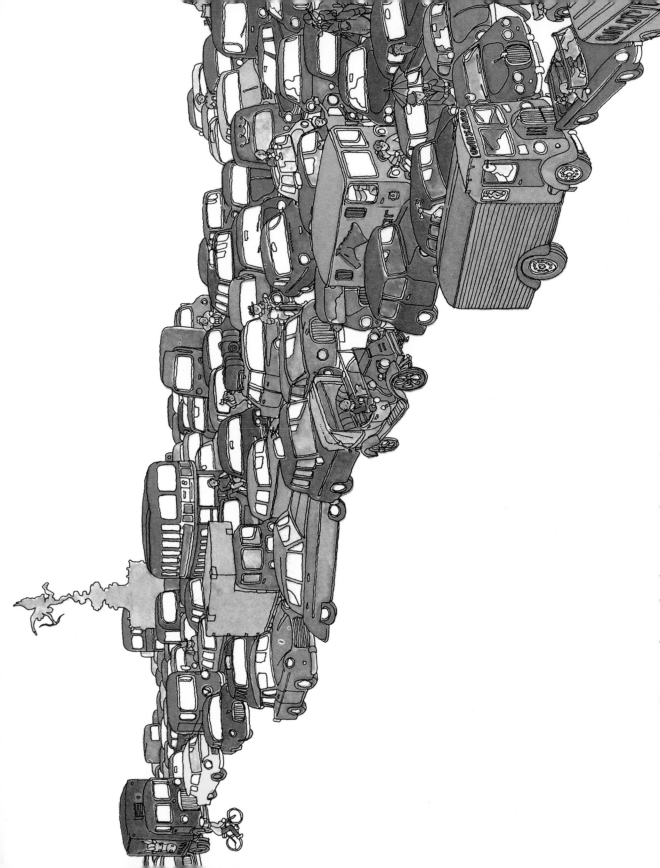

Cars and trucks, buses and taxis, bicycles and motorbikes jam the streets of London. One of the most crowded places in the city is called Piccadilly Circus. (In England a "circus" is a circle or square where a number of streets meet.) At Piccadilly, six of London's busiest streets come together around a statue of Eros, the Greek god of love. He seems to float over the intersection with his drawn bow.

At Piccadilly you never have to look far to find one of London's famous, bright red double-decker buses. London buses are different from those of most other cities. They have an upstairs and a downstairs. Narrow, winding stairs lead to the upper deck. It is not easy to climb up if the bus is going fast, but once you reach the top you have a wonderful view. You can look down on office workers, store windows, and pedestrians.

There are often big traffic jams like this at Piccadilly Circus. But they aren't always caused by a family of dachshunds trying to get across the street. However, in London people love their pets so much that a policeman thinks nothing of stopping traffic so a family of dogs can cross the road safely.

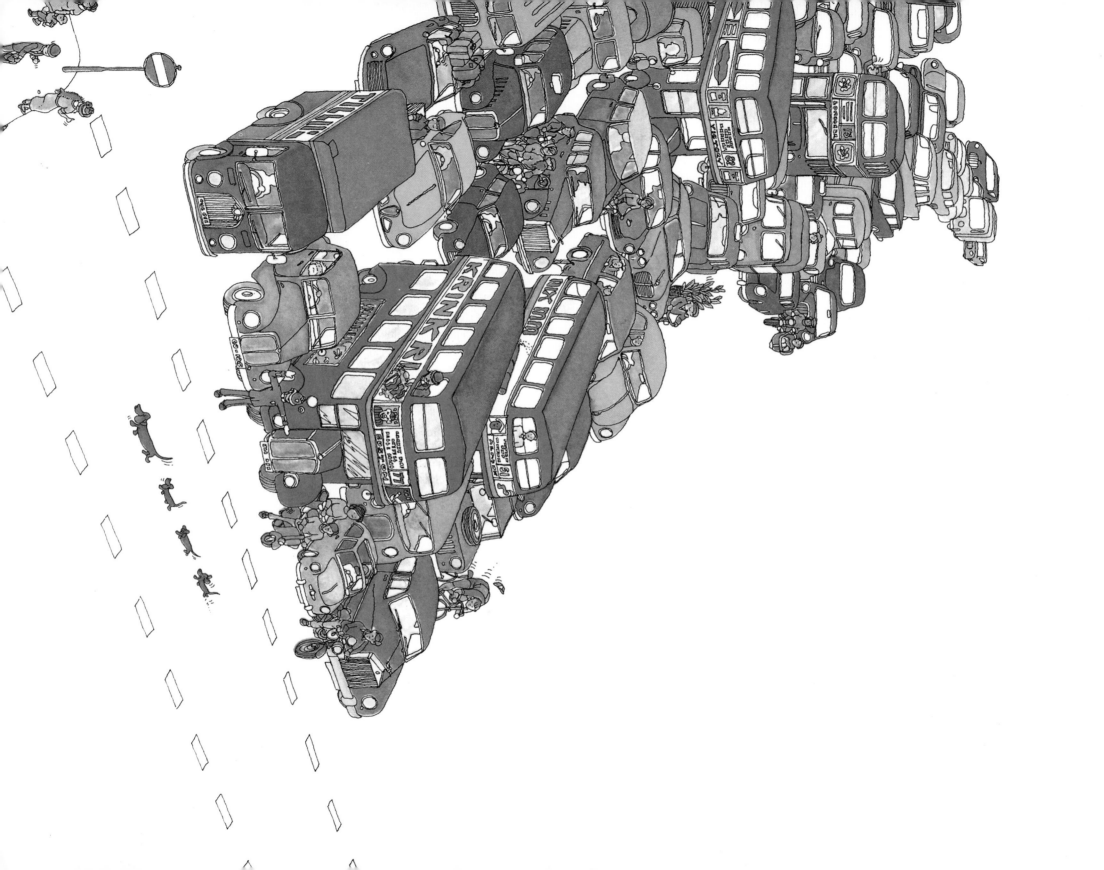

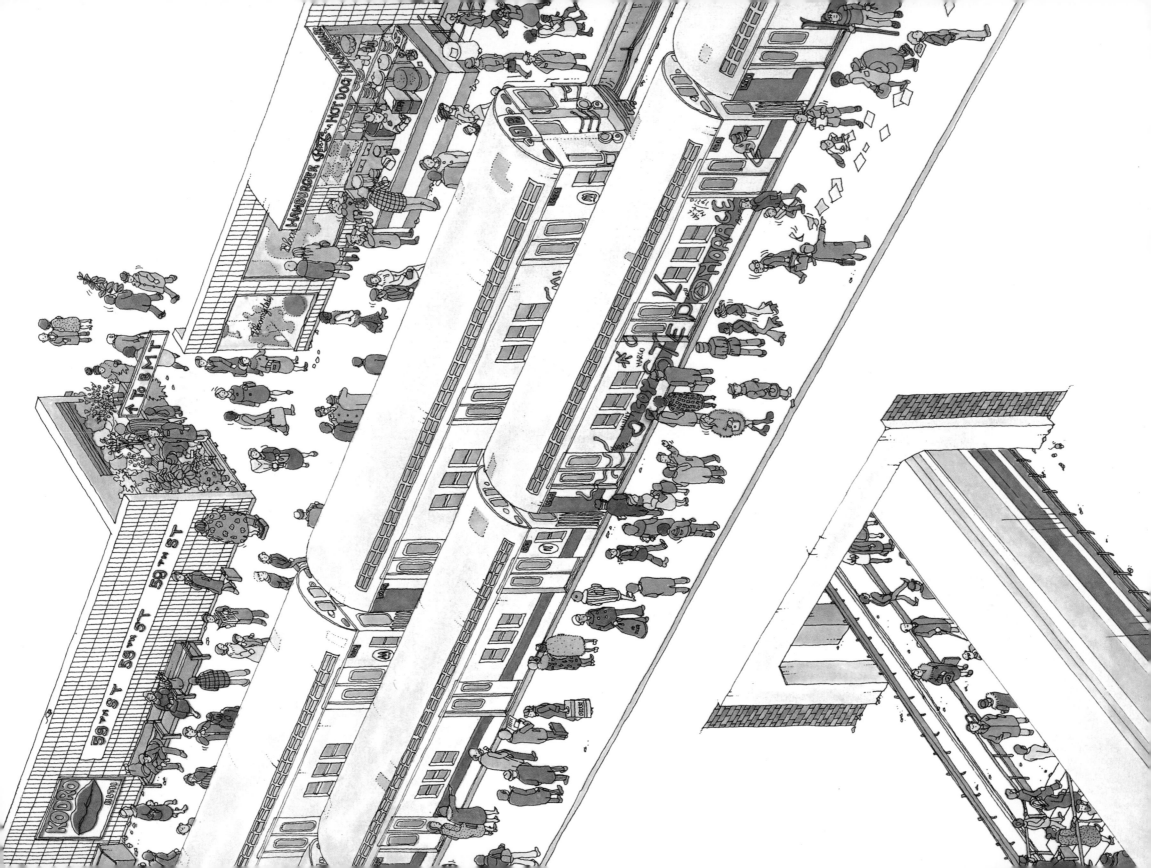

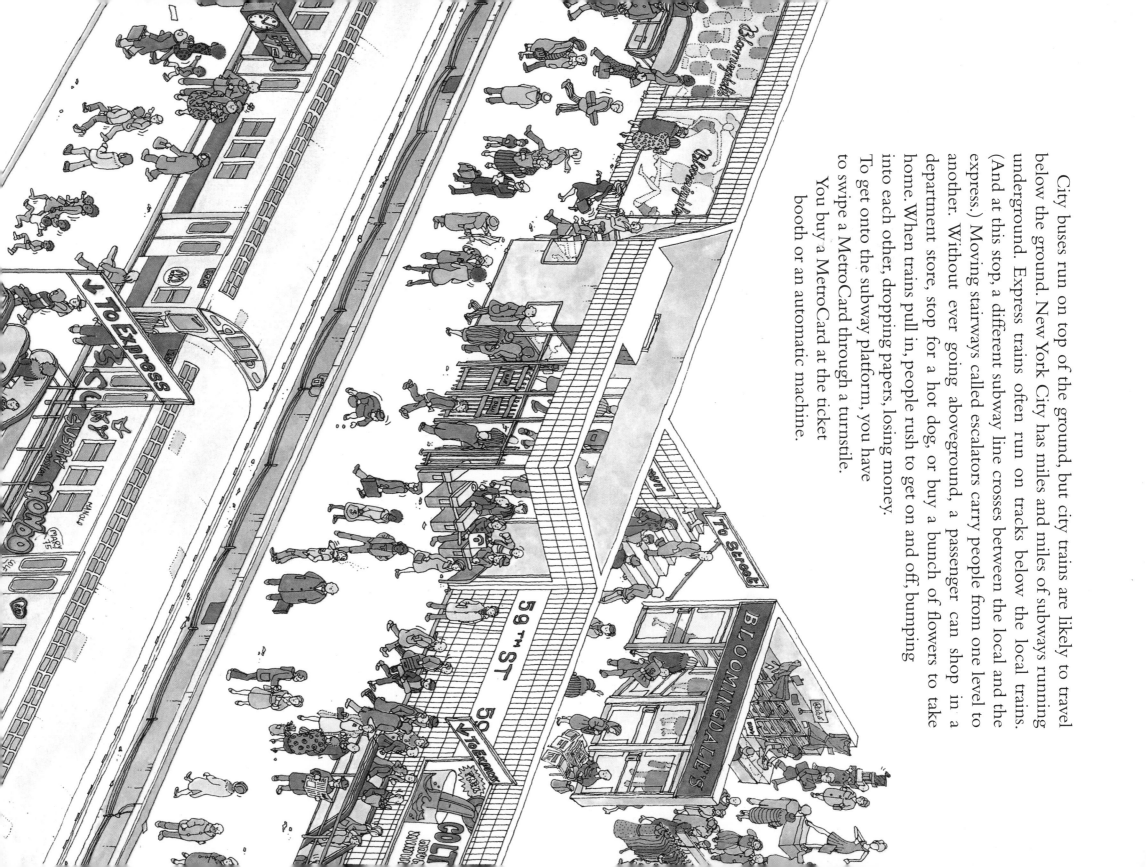

City buses run on top of the ground, but city trains are likely to travel below the ground. New York City has miles and miles of subways running underground. Express trains often run on tracks below the local trains. (And at this stop, a different subway line crosses between the local and the express.) Moving stairways called escalators carry people from one level to another. Without ever going aboveground, a passenger can shop in a department store, stop for a hot dog, or buy a bunch of flowers to take home. When trains pull in, people rush to get on and off, bumping into each other, dropping papers, losing money.

To get onto the subway platform, you have to swipe a MetroCard through a turnstile. You buy a MetroCard at the ticket booth or an automatic machine.

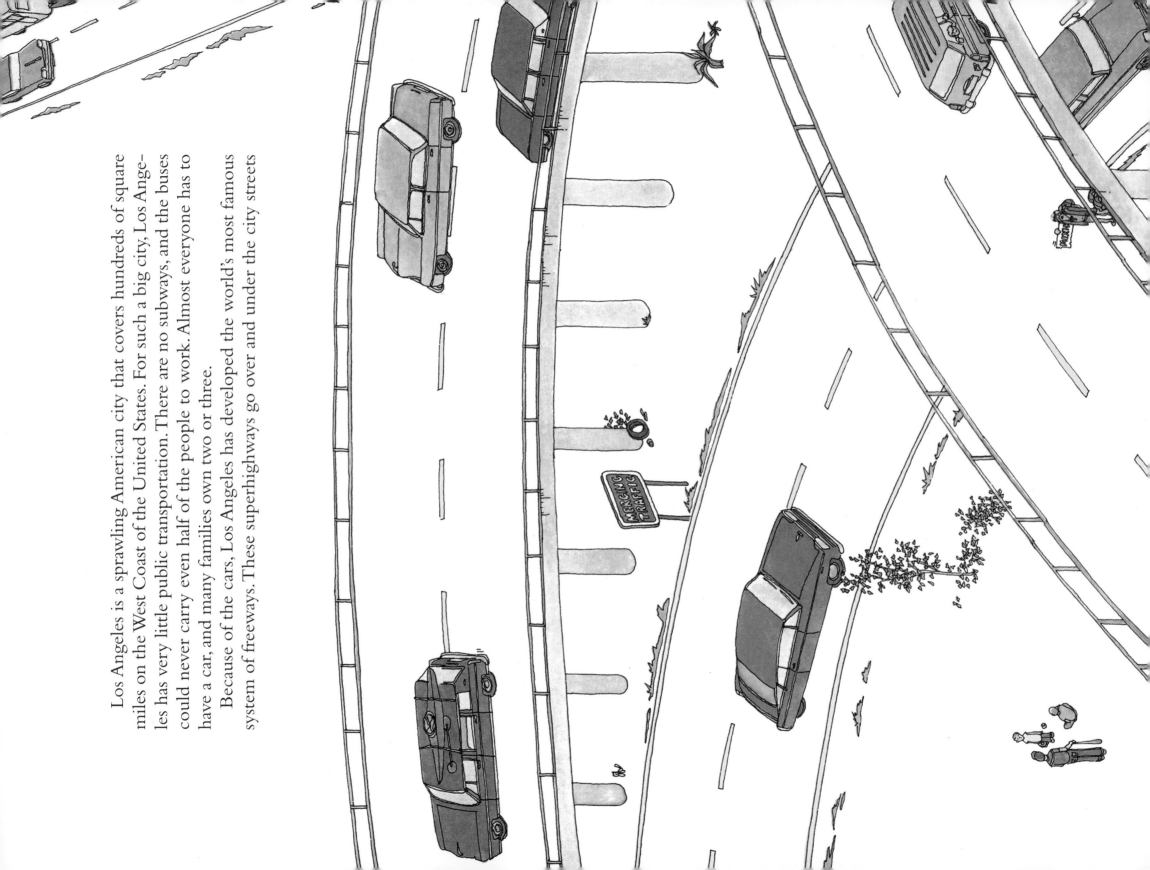

Los Angeles is a sprawling American city that covers hundreds of square miles on the West Coast of the United States. For such a big city, Los Angeles has very little public transportation. There are no subways, and the buses could never carry even half of the people to work. Almost everyone has to have a car, and many families own two or three.

Because of the cars, Los Angeles has developed the world's most famous system of freeways. These superhighways go over and under the city streets

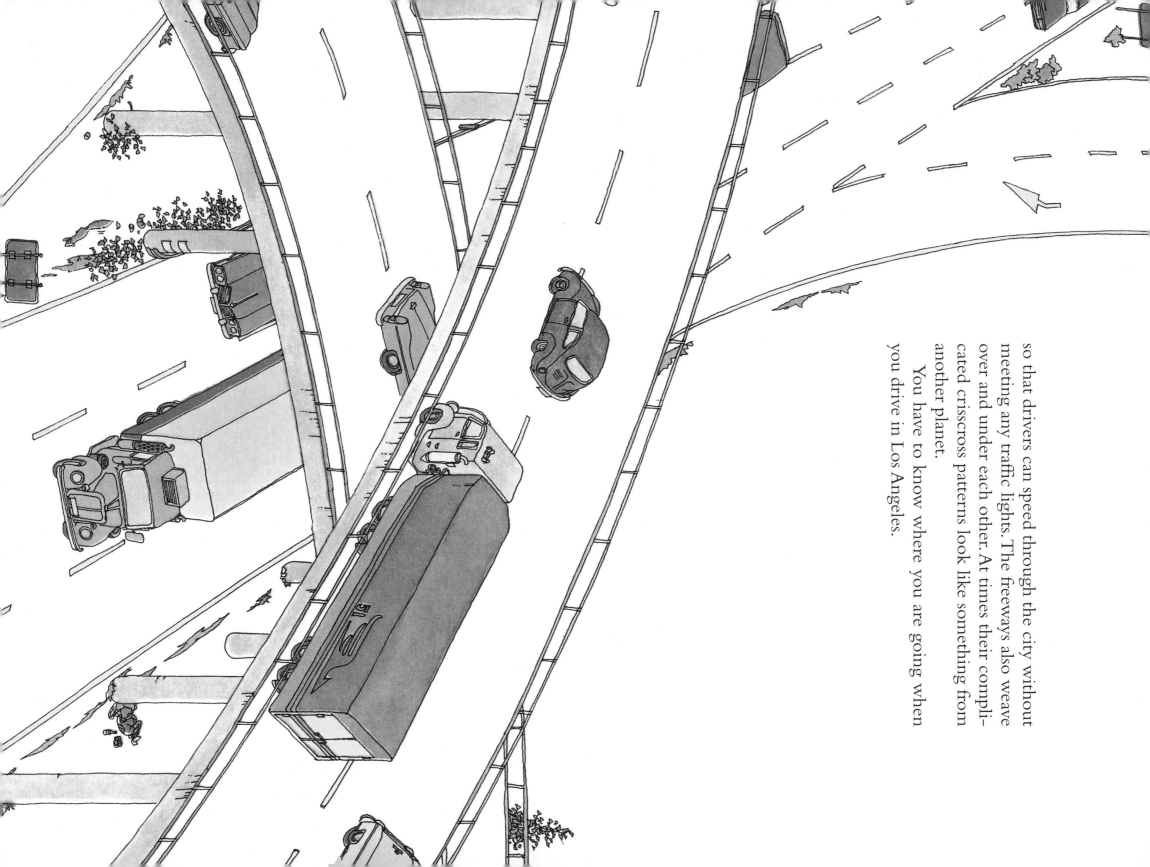

so that drivers can speed through the city without meeting any traffic lights. The freeways also weave over and under each other. At times their complicated crisscross patterns look like something from another planet.

You have to know where you are going when you drive in Los Angeles.

In Italy there is a city where *nobody* rides in cars or trucks or taxis. This city is built on islands, and canals take the place of roads. The people who live here have to travel by boat. The name of this city is Venice, and it is one of the loveliest places in the world.

At one time, everybody in Venice traveled in flat-bottomed boats called gondolas. A gondolier with a long oar acted as a chauffeur. But today most

people travel in modern motorboats. Venice is a city of lovely old churches, beautiful bridges, and busy shops and outdoor markets. One section of the city is built on the mainland where there are cars and roads, but on the islands no one ever sees a car.

The industrial cities of Germany do not look much like Venice. In places like Essen and Dusseldorf, hundreds of people work in factories and live in homes outside the city limits. They have to ride to work on trains. These trains are not subways. They run aboveground, sometimes above the streets so they won't interfere with traffic.

At the end of the day, the workers stream out of the factories. Some get into cars and drive home, but most of them take the train.

HAWAII
WARTET
SIE!

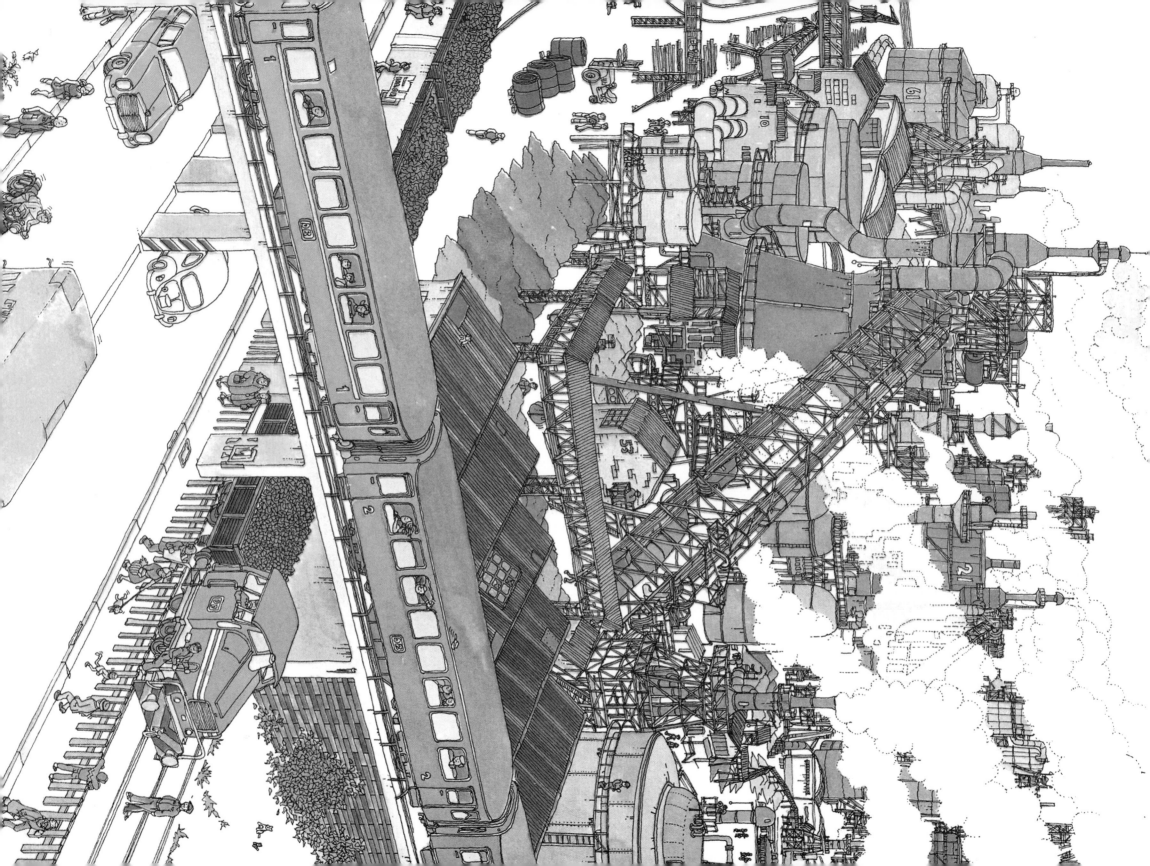

WORKING IN A CITY

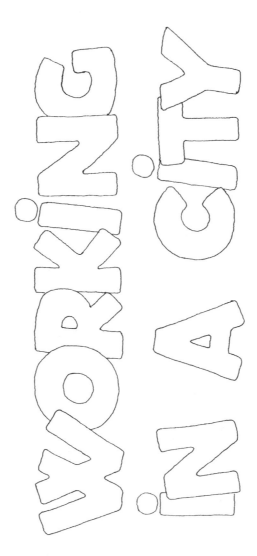

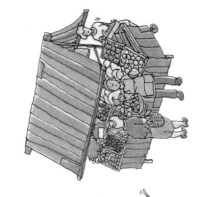

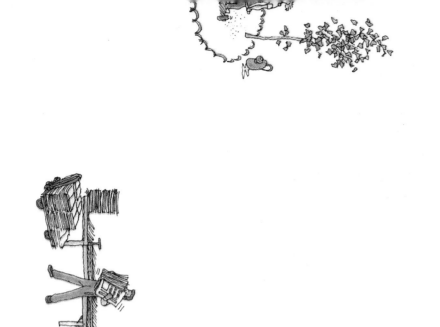

During the past fifty years, more and more people have moved to cities. There are many reasons for this, and one of the most important is the number and variety of jobs available. Most manufacturing takes place in or near cities, so thousands of people are needed to work in factories. Then there are the people needed for running the city itself: police, firemen, teachers, hospital personnel, sanitation and transportation workers—the list is endless.

The stores, financial centers, and places of amusement also require big staffs. The unusual job opportunities attract young people from all over, and the stimulating atmosphere ensures that cities have more than their share of skilled craftsmen, artists, and creative people of all sorts.

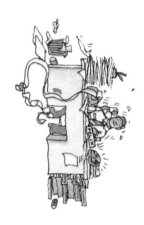

Among the people who work for the city are the firemen. They have a very important job to do. Fires are especially dangerous in a city because the buildings stand so close together. If a big fire ever got out of control it could spread all over the city.

Stockholm, the capital of Sweden, has a very modern and efficient fire department. There are big hook-and-ladder trucks that can drive up alongside a burning building and raise long extension ladders for firemen to use in rescuing people trapped by the flames. Or the firemen can climb up the ladders with their long hoses. Water trucks supply water to pump through these hoses. The fire-department officers ride in long sedans painted bright red like the fire trucks.

Throughout the city the fire department has set up alarm boxes for people to use to report fires. The call goes directly to Central Alarm in Greater Stockholm, and firefighters from the nearest stations rush to the danger spot in a matter of minutes. There are nine stations located throughout the city and usually firemen from at least two stations answer every call.

Like policemen and sanitation workers, the firemen are important for the safety and well-being of a city.

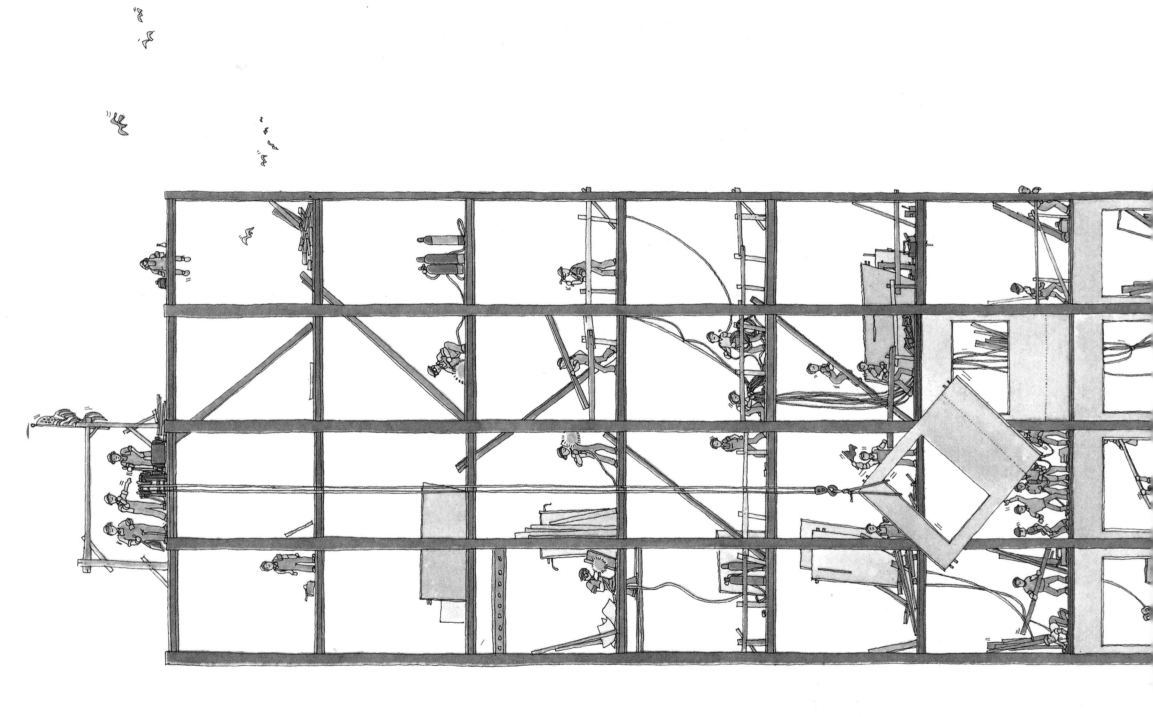

In every city there are always men at work putting up new buildings. Often the buildings are tall skyscrapers. Because property is very expensive in the city, it is cheaper to build straight up into the air instead of spreading out over a lot of land. Huge cranes raise the steel girders to the top of a new building. Men pour concrete for floors that will make the buildings fireproof. Aluminum or glass siding gives protection from wind and rain. Sometimes the lower part of a skyscraper is nearly finished while men are just beginning work on the upper part.

At first skyscrapers were most common in American cities, but now you will find them in any big city where the land is solid enough to support them.

Thousands of people swarm into these tall buildings every morning. They may be doctors or dentists, artists or engineers. Many of the workers sit at desks, writing e-mails or directing company business. Others work at computers or carry important papers from one office to another. All day long men and women come and go, holding meetings, figuring out how to do difficult jobs, running all the different kinds of office machines.

Many big skyscrapers are cities in themselves, complete with stores, restaurants, and theaters—and even apartments.

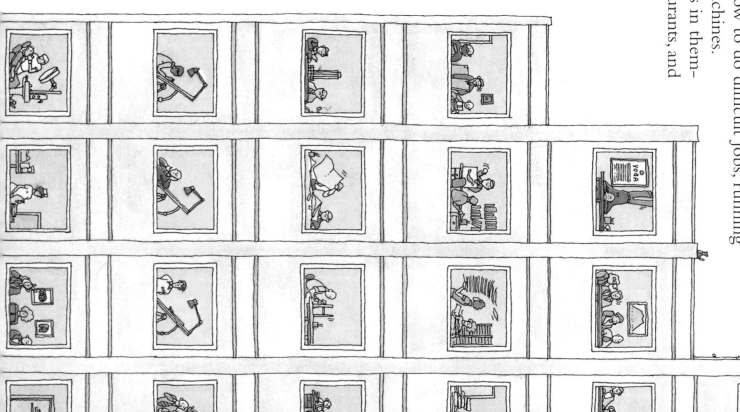

The New York City Stock Exchange is the largest stock exchange in the world. It is also the most famous financial institution in the United States—often referred to as "the nation's marketplace."

Here, on a vast trading floor, hundreds of exchange members daily buy and sell, for thousands of people all over the world, the stocks and bonds of most of America's leading corporations. Since a share of stock is a share of a company, the Stock Exchange enables people to buy an interest in any company listed on the exchange.

Thousands of visitors come to the exchange every year to watch, from an overhead gallery, the constant rushing about of people on the trading floor. As sales are made, the "Big Board" that overlooks the busy floor flashes the latest prices. Computers and 500,000 miles of teletype and telephone wires tabulate the sales and connect buyers and purchasers all over the country.

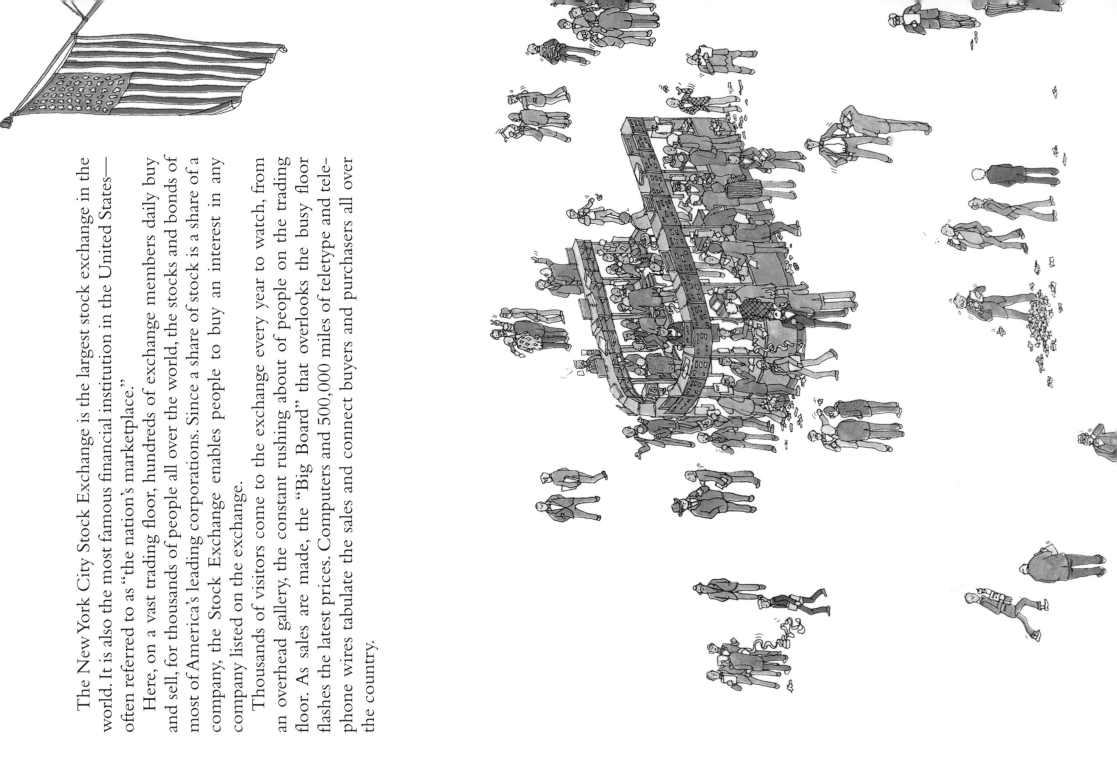

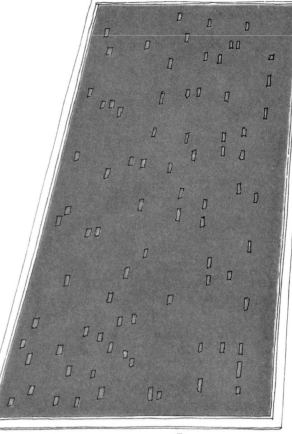
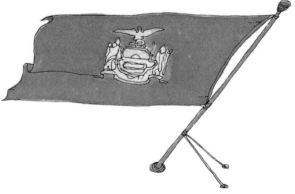

Thousands of city people work in stores. All day long they help busy shoppers find what they have come to buy. It is fun to go shopping in big cities because the huge stores are filled with so many different things. Department stores like Au Printemps in Paris, France, carry everything from neckties to sailboats. You can order the latest model car, buy a new dress, or pick out new furniture. (The clerks will even let you try out a bed—but don't fall asleep on it!) Long escalators move the customers from one floor to another. At Au Printemps you will find a big assortment of champagne and perfume, two of the things for which France is especially famous.

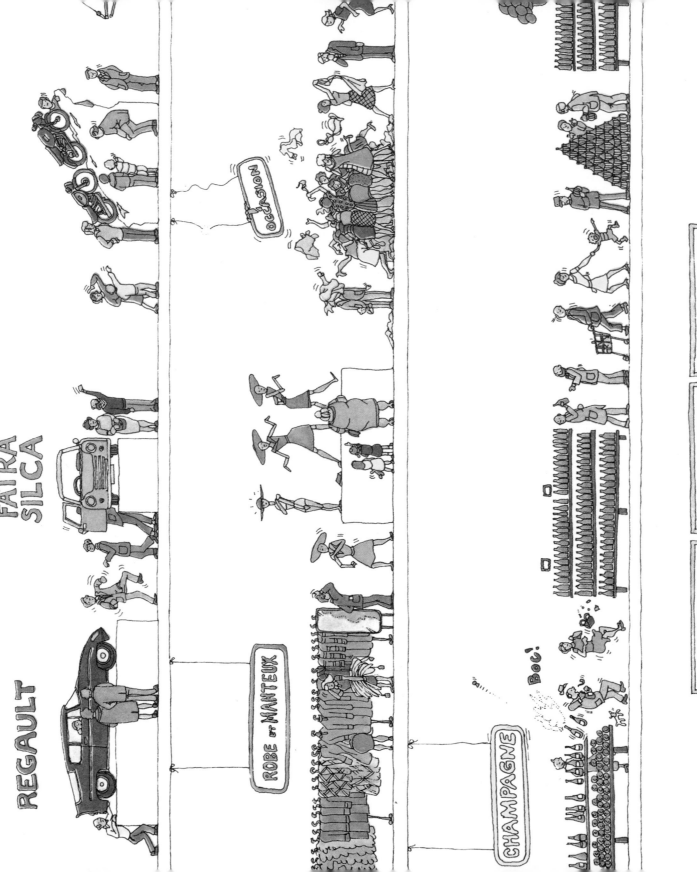

REGAULT

FATRA SILCA

ROBE et MANTEUX

OCCASION

CHAMPAGNE

Boc!

ENTRÉE   SORTIE   ENTRÉE

TABACS

LE FIGARO
FRANCE SOIR   L'ÉQUIPE
VOGUE LE MONDE
PARIS MATCH TINTIN
COMBAT MARIE CLAIRE

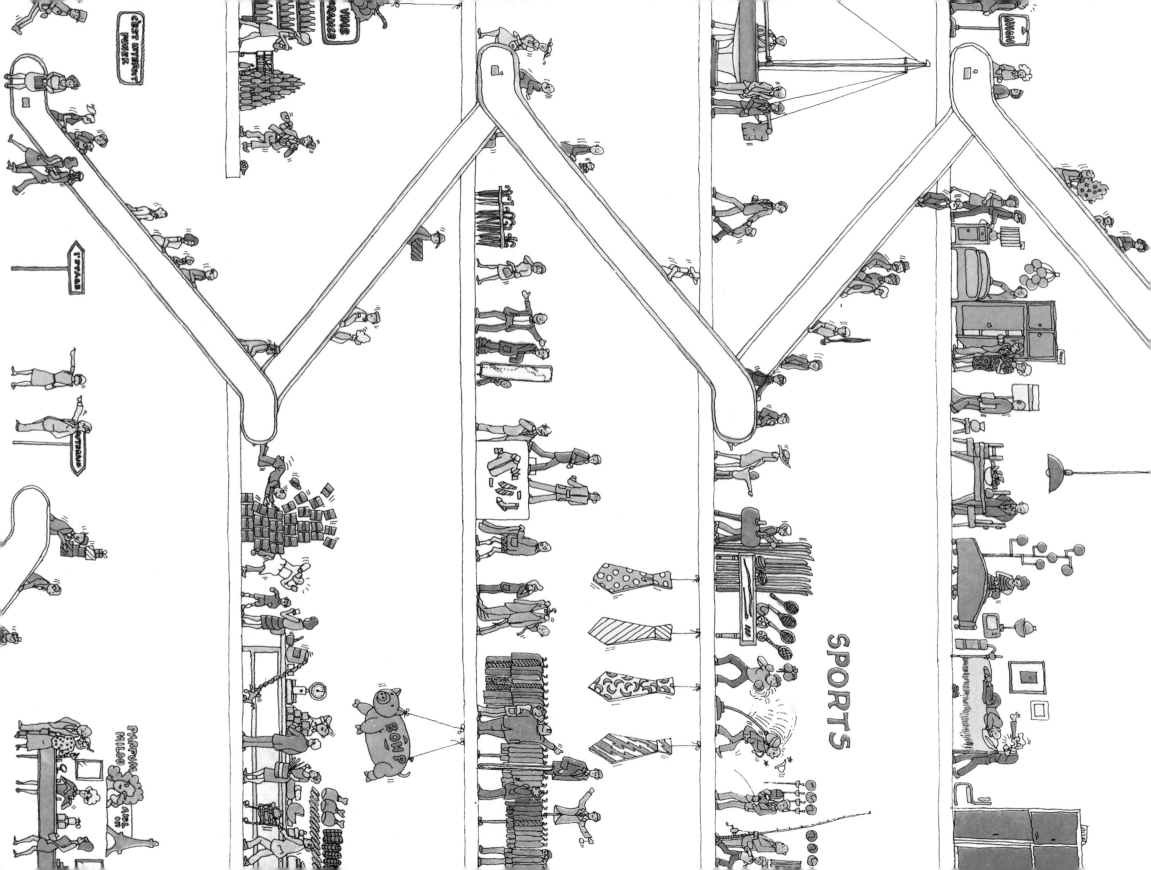

There are also "department stores" that are outdoors. You will find many of these in the Middle East. Here, for hundreds of years, merchants have gathered to display their wares in outdoor markets. They come into the center of the cities with their amazing assortment of merchandise packed on camels and donkeys. You can find almost anything you want if you look hard enough—clothing, jewelry, carpets; even an old sewing machine or a clothes dryer. Nobody expects you to pay the asking price. You have to bargain. And you can look at an article as long as you like. In fact, you can even try it out. A lot of the things for sale may be worthless, but a shrewd shopper can often find some real bargains and wonderful curiosities. If you get bored with shopping, there are usually jugglers, fire-eaters, or snake charmers to entertain you.

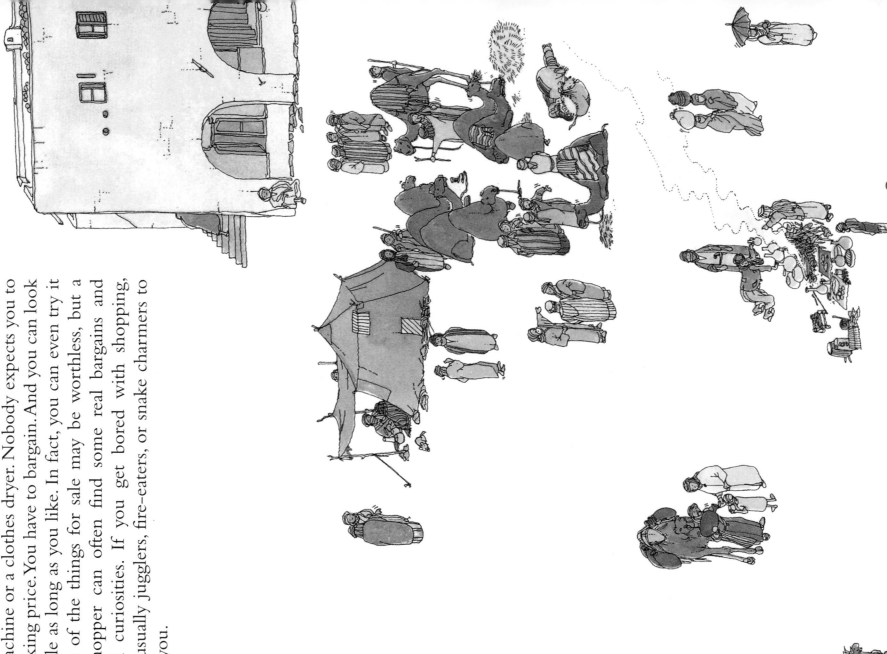

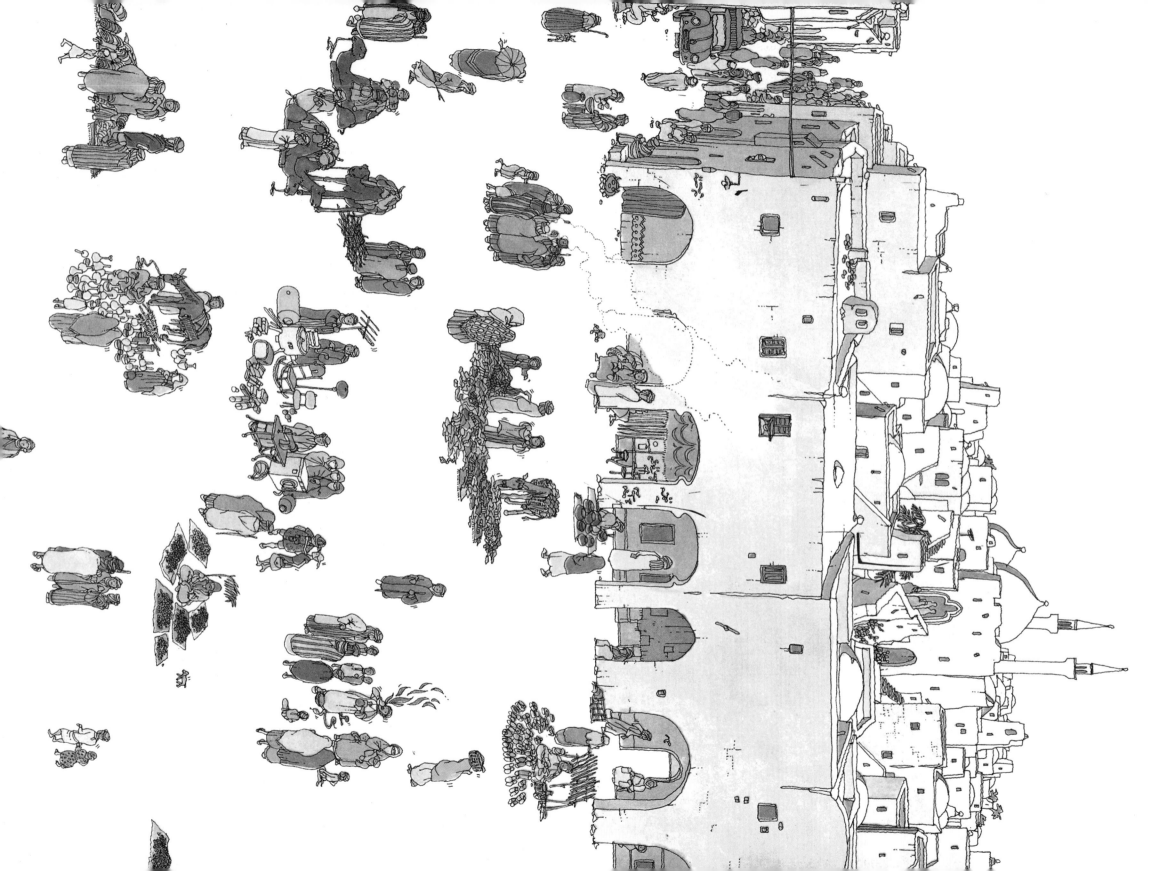

This is the harbor at Hamburg, Germany, one of the largest seaports in Europe. Hamburg is a perfect port because it is located on two lakes and two rivers, as well as a whole system of canals. One of the rivers, the Elbe, provides it with easy access to the North Sea. It is also one of the leading railroad centers in Germany.

The port section of a city has a life all its own. It has a special traffic system, and the dockside workers have their own way of talking and doing things. Tugboats lead the big freighters into the harbor. Tall cranes unload all the goods that are packed into these floating storehouses, and fill them up again with new freight for their next stop. There are special police to supervise the harbor, and all kinds of freight cars and barges to carry goods to and from the busy waterfront.

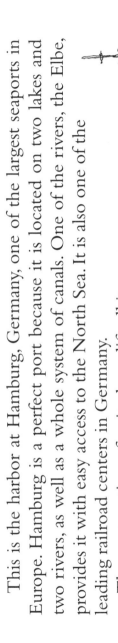

HAVING FUN IN A CITY

FUN FUN CITY

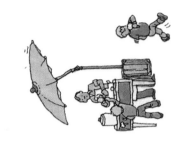

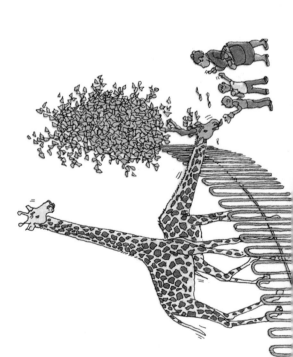

Cities are wonderful places for having fun. When the weather is good, people stroll on the streets, go window-shopping in front of big stores, or have picnics in the park. Many cities have zoos with exotic animals. And professional teams play sports like baseball, football, soccer, and basketball. (Amateur players—both old and young— have their own games on school playgrounds or in the city parks.)

Big cities are also great cultural centers with museums full of paintings and fascinating historical treasures. There are museums that feature science and animal life, and planetariums for learning about the stars and planets.

Most cities also have theaters for stage plays as well as motion pictures, and there are usually concerts to attend. Often a band or orchestra will give a free concert in a park. Whether the weather is good or bad, you can always find a way to amuse yourself in a city.

There are more than 1,700 parks in New York City. Some are big, others are small. But all of them provide a place for people to get away from stuffy buildings and enjoy the outdoors. The best-known is Central Park. Located right in the center of Manhattan (the central borough of the city), it covers 843 acres. There are fields for playing ball, playgrounds for younger children, and wooded areas where birds are safe to nest and raise families. Many people go rowing on the lake, and horse lovers ride on the bridle path. Here one of the riders is on a footpath. Probably the mounted policeman will tell her to take the horse back where he belongs! There are parts of Central Park that don't seem to be in a city at all. If you couldn't see the skyscrapers peeking over the trees, you might think you were in the country.

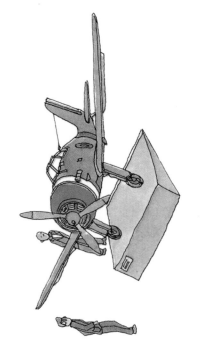

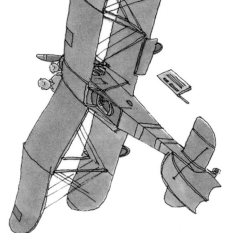

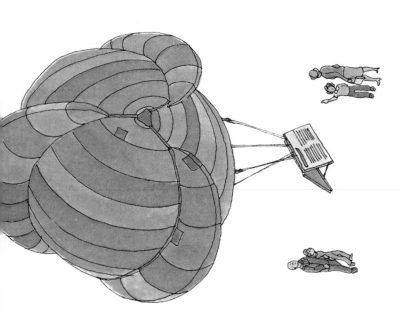

On rainy days it's fun to visit museums—institutions that collect and display original objects.

In Washington, D.C., the Smithsonian Institution collects and shows many different kinds of things. One of its divisions, the National Air and Space Museum, records American achievements in air and space flight. There you can see the Kitty Hawk, the first airplane built and actually flown by the Wright Brothers, and the Spirit of St. Louis, which carried Charles Lindbergh on the first nonstop flight from America to Europe.

Another popular branch of the Smithsonian shows exhibits of fossils, minerals, plants, and animals—including reconstructions of dinosaurs and other prehistoric creatures.

The Metropolitan Museum in New York City, on the other hand, concentrates on objects of art. One of its most fascinating exhibits is the hall of armor, where you can see the swords and heavy metal armor worn by knights and horses in the Middle Ages.

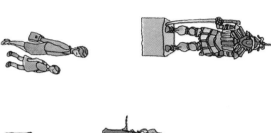

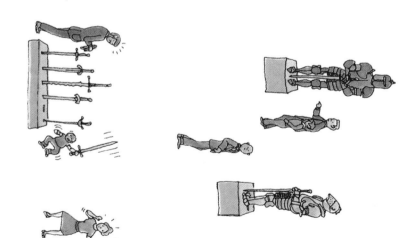

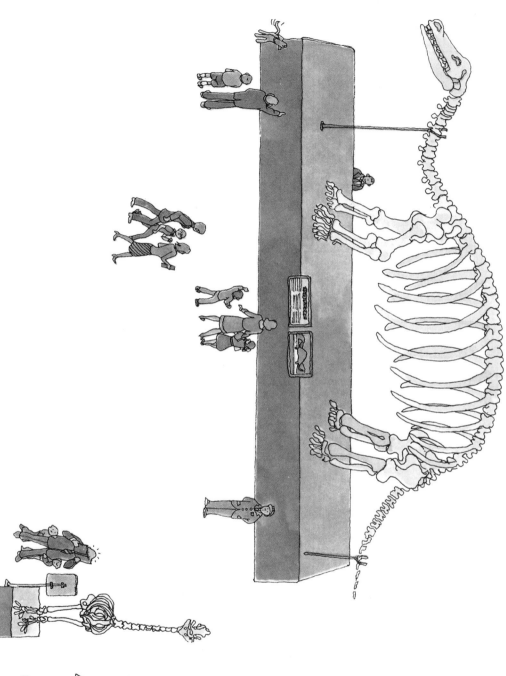

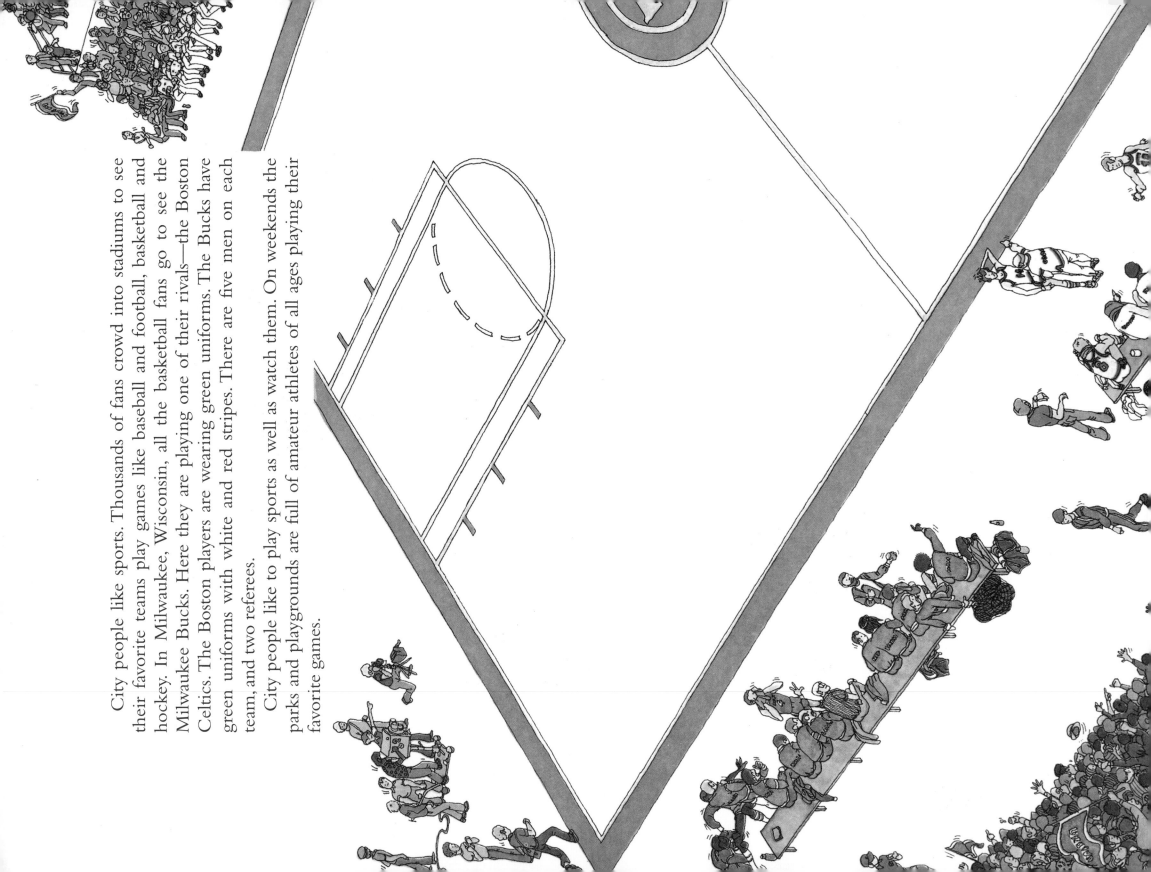

City people like sports. Thousands of fans crowd into stadiums to see their favorite teams play games like baseball and football, basketball and hockey. In Milwaukee, Wisconsin, all the basketball fans go to see the Milwaukee Bucks. Here they are playing one of their rivals—the Boston Celtics. The Boston players are wearing green uniforms. The Bucks have green uniforms with white and red stripes. There are five men on each team, and two referees.

City people like to play sports as well as watch them. On weekends the parks and playgrounds are full of amateur athletes of all ages playing their favorite games.

In Tokyo, and a few other Japanese cities, people go to see a different kind of sport called *sumo*. This unusual kind of wrestling has been practiced for many centuries.

The ring is fifteen feet in diameter, and it is set on a two-foot-high mound of hard clay. The wrestlers wear heavy silk belts thirty feet long and about two feet wide. The referee is dressed in a gleaming kimono and carries a little paddle for signaling.

The object of sumo wrestling is to force the other man out of the ring, or make him touch the ground inside the ring with any part of his body except the soles of his feet. A wrestler may try to grab his opponent's belt and lift him, or he may simply slap and shove him. Many of these wrestlers are huge. If a man weighs enough, he is very difficult to force out of the ring. Sumo wrestlers as young as sixteen often weigh as much as 350 pounds! The spectators close to the ring sit on cushions or delicate straw mats, and always remove their shoes. Sometimes 13,000 fans crowd around to watch the sumo matches. Others watch at home on their television sets.

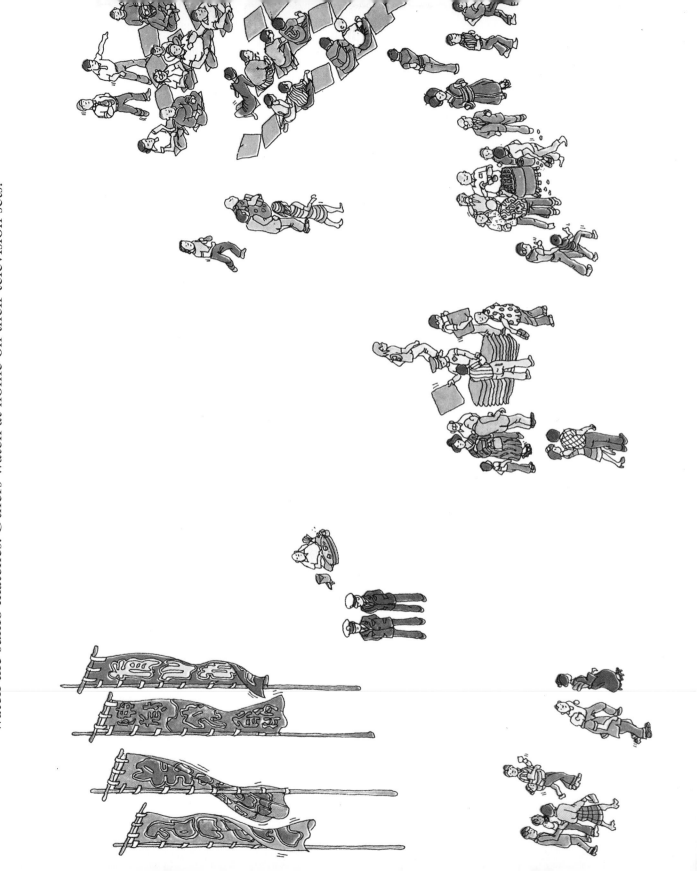

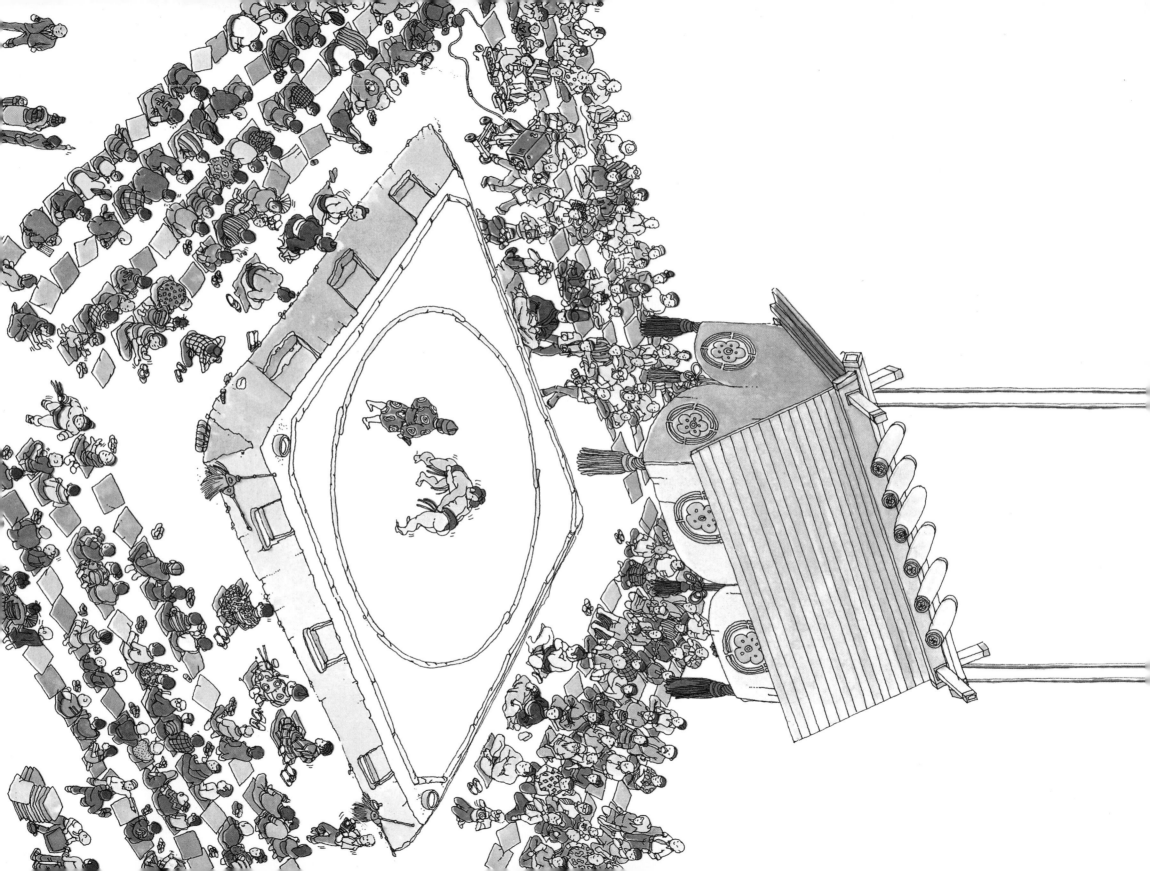

City people also go to the theater for entertainment. They can see plays and movies, and go to concerts and operas. One of the most famous theaters in the world is La Scala Opera House in Milan, Italy. Every opera singer hopes to be invited someday to sing at La Scala. The auditorium is beautiful, with red-plush seats, white and gold paint, and six tiers of boxes gracefully rising to the ceiling.

The stage is so huge that even an elephant and a team of horses can come onstage for the triumphal march in Verdi's famous opera *Aida*. The setting for the opera is ancient Egypt. You can tell just by looking at the figures painted on the scenery and the costumes that the singers are wearing.

There is a conductor to lead the orchestra; and, peeking out from a little opening in the middle of the footlights, is a director who prompts the singers if they forget their lines or their stage positions.

Cities are wonderful places for walking and sightseeing. In Paris people enjoy strolling along the banks of the River Seine. On the Left Bank there are rows of open-air bookstalls, really long boxes resting on the wall that borders the river. These bookstalls have lined the sidewalk for more than 300 years. In them, you will find second-hand books, old postcards, prints, maps, stamps, coins, and even medals. Once in a great while, if you search long enough, you can find a real treasure.

If you get tired of browsing, you can look across the river to the beautiful Notre Dame Cathedral with its square towers and pointed spires. Or you can watch a barge carrying freight past the tip of the island on which the cathedral is located.

On a sunny day children play along the riverside and mothers push baby carriages past artists who are trying to sell their paintings.

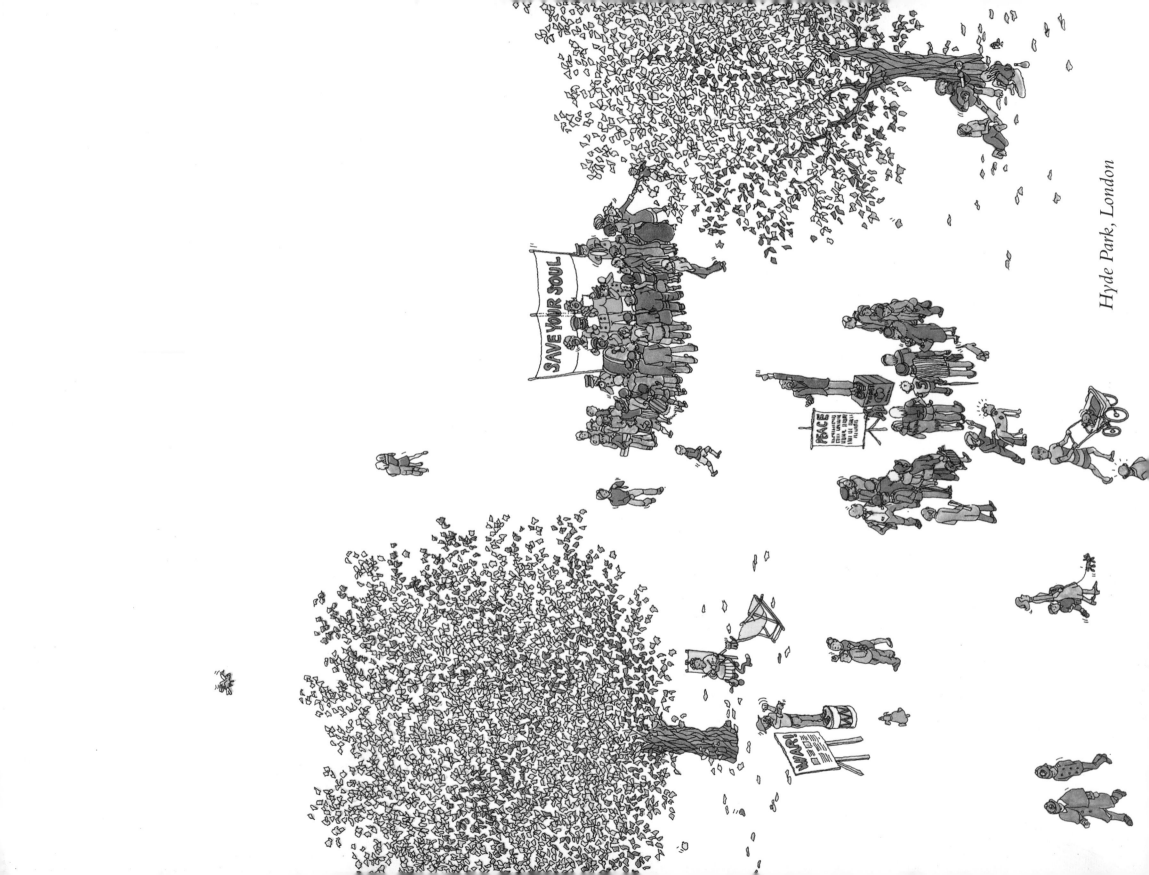